Narcissism

Recognize And Comprehend The Narcissistic Individual In Your Existence To Get Enduring Tranquilly

(Narcissistic Personality Disorder: The Inequivalve Guide)

Karim Fournier

TABLE OF CONTENT

An Anthology Of Narcissistic Storytelling..................... 1

Ways To Recognise Narcissism... 7

Applying The Grey Rock Approach...............................25

Sensitivity And Narcissism: An Unspoken Paradox 42

Comprehending And Getting Past Grief.......................69

How To Coexist With An Idiostrophic.........................94

Fundamental Ideas On Narcissism............................116

An Anthology Of Narcissistic Storytelling

This chapter will go deeply into the historical narratives and folklore that have quietly shaped our collective perception of narcissistic persons by painting vivid pictures of their characteristics. You'll discover that narcissism has long been intertwined into the fabric of humanity as we unravel these tales.

However, before this historical voyage, let's pause to consider something crucial: You're not alone in your quest for healing and self-discovery. Numerous people have struggled with the intricacies of narcissistic relationships, just like you. Although it might be simple to feel alone, keep in mind that you are part of a larger group of resilient people who are survivors and seekers who are committed to escaping unhealthy relationships.

This chapter aims to illuminate the historical roots of narcissism as it has been portrayed, rather than to pass judgment or assign labels. Understanding how these stories have influenced our views may help you better grasp the causes of this mysterious personality condition.

Along the process, we'll also be posing some difficult issues that may cause you to reevaluate your understanding of narcissism.

Now, let's go back in time and examine the myths and stories that shaped our knowledge of narcissism. You will learn that information is the first step towards liberty and that the Echo of narcissistic qualities has long echoed through the halls of history as we go through the ages.

Legends and Myths

Let's delve into the interesting realm of narcissistic characters found in old myths and stories. It's crucial to keep in mind that narcissism as a notion precedes the contemporary clinical understanding of narcissistic personality disorder when we examine these stories. In these tales, narcissism frequently takes the form of extreme self-love, conceit, and an obsession with one's wishes and image.

The Greek myth of Narcissus is among the most well-known instances of narcissism. Narcissus was a very attractive young man who was loved by many, according to Ovid's "Metamorphoses," but he was completely self-absorbed and uninterested in other people's feelings for him. The terrible turn in his tale occurs when he falls in love with his reflection in a pool of water. He can't help but stare at his reflection until he passes out from his intense affection for it. Because of this narrative, the word "narcissism" itself comes from the name of Narcissus (Gillette, 2017).

The tale of Echo and Narcissus is another Greek myth that discusses narcissism. A curse prevents Echo, a nymph with a lovely voice, from expressing her feelings for Narcissus when she falls in love. Instead, she can only repeat other people's words. Because of Narcissus's self-centeredness, Echo is rejected, which ultimately results in her death. As we saw in the preceding tale, the gods punish Narcissus by causing him to fall in love with his reflection (Gillette, 2017).

There is a story in Norse mythology about a narcissistic figure named Loki. Although he is well-known for his slyness and capacity to change shape, Loki also exhibits narcissistic tendencies. In the tale of Loki's Flyting, a poetic back-and-forth of insults, Loki disparages the other gods while bragging about his many achievements. His conceit and excessive self-praise cause him to argue with other gods (Gillette, 2017).

Beyond the confines of the West, myths and legends from other civilizations contain three instances of narcissism:

In Indian mythology, narcissism In Hindu mythology, the narcissistic interpretation of Ravana from the epic Ramayana is common. His narcissistic characteristics are highlighted by his love with Princess Sita and his conviction that he deserves her, even after she rejects him (Majumdar, 2022).

Chinese mythology on narcissism: The fabled beauty Xi Shi is supposed to have brought down an entire kingdom because of her narcissistic charms. Her narrative highlights the strength of conceit and its potentially disastrous effects (Cai et al., 2011).

Egyptian mythology's narcissism: Although there isn't a clear link between it and Narcissus, the Pharaohs, who frequently thought of themselves as a god, may have possessed narcissistic qualities. Their overwhelming self-love is seen in their infatuation with monuments and grandeur (Taub, 2023).

These myths are meant to act as a warning about the damaging effects of narcissism. They draw attention to the negative effects of self-obsession, such as loneliness, rejection, and even tragic outcomes. Additionally, they offer insightful perspectives on the human condition since narcissism is still a pertinent issue in modern psychology and culture. Examining these antiquated tales can aid in our comprehension of the persistent effects of narcissism on people and cultures across time.

Ways To Recognise Narcissism

Has anyone you've dated shown a strong interest in you? They bring you gifts, surprise you at work, shower you with presents, and perhaps even treat you to opulent vacations! But all of a sudden, everything just stops. They either don't pick up the phone or neglect you for a few days, blaming it on family issues, work obligations, or general busyness.

They return to their excessively romantic ways after seeming sincere in their apology. The performance begins with presents, special occasions, and tender surprises. But then there is a little period of complete quiet. What took place? This is known as "love bombing," my friends. You're perplexed by your partner's quiet. You start to doubt yourself, which is the one thing they would have expected you to do.

You start to question whether you made a mistake. Additionally, you start to question whether you are overreacting and justify your actions by reasoning that since the person you are dating seems to be genuinely interested in you, you must be the one who is at fault. This is not true at all because the issue is not with you. The issue is with them. This is a game that this individual is engaged in, and all narcissists enjoy playing since it gives them a sense of control. They take great pleasure in their seemingly limitless control over the other person. It's almost like going on a power trip.

You are probably dealing with a narcissist if you have ever encountered the situation I just described. Healthy, caring, honest, and empathic people won't engage in this unstable game. Rather, they feel obligated to give you a call or send you a text. They don't abruptly stop talking to you and get in touch with you after four days. The narcissist, however, does not end there. Sadly, things get worse.

Have you ever seen your partner do something, only to have them deny it when you bring it up? Have you heard them say something as obvious as day, and when you challenge them, their first reaction is always denial? One of the main characteristics of a narcissist is denial. They'll contest your existence. You seem to have to keep proving your point until they acknowledge and own up to their mistakes, but that acceptance never materializes. One of their favorite tools for keeping you in circles and keeping them secure is denial.

The first thing that springs to mind when someone thinks about narcissism is self-centeredness and vanity. These are only the outward manifestations of narcissism; deep-seated behaviors extend beyond them and include, among other things, patterns of denial, gaslighting, love bombing, grandiosity, entitlement, control, and a lack of empathy and validation.

The feeling that you are insufficient is the most damaging consequence of living with a narcissist. When you go above and beyond to make your spouse change or show appreciation for you, no matter how hard you work to keep your home clean, exercise, cut your hair, look nice, or prepare home-cooked meals, you know you are dating or married to a narcissist. Thus, you fall into the trap of believing that your sweetness or increased love for them will bring about change.

You have this fantasy of the beast and the beauty, believing that if you love someone more, they will transform into the kind, sincere, and perceptive companion you have always imagined. Unfortunately, since narcissism is a collection of actions that have been ingrained in a person since childhood, it is nothing more than wishful thinking. It isn't even apparent to narcissists that they need to change. Many studies and publications indicate that they won't and that it wastes time and effort.

For those of you who are the targets of narcissism, it might be discouraging to try and alter your partner despite your best efforts to be all that you can be. You will become weary of the lack of empathy. It is in our nature as humans to want to be heard and understood. However, there is no compassion for your suffering, despair, or annoyance if you are with a narcissistic spouse. The narcissist will blame you and turn the tables on you. They are skilled at assigning blame and making you feel like the source of all the conflict in the relationship.

You cannot be born a narcissist. They grow up. In what way? The following components come together to provide the framework for narcissistic behaviors. A youngster who had emotional maltreatment and unmet needs as a child could develop into a narcissistic adult. A youngster who had to earn their parent's love and attention via their scholastic achievements is beginning to realize that love is something you have to earn and is not always given. You have the prodigal child gifted in every endeavor, including athletics. On the outside, you can see their parents applauding from the stands and showing off their awards and academic accomplishments, but when the child needs emotional support, you can never find their parents. To put it another way, it is not unconditional but conditional.

The emotional environment of a youngster is neglected and unsupervised. A child's identity and basic being become more shallow when their emotions are treated with less respect. Resulting in the development of traits like grandiosity, attention-seeking, and the need for validation. Even though narcissists—some of them, perhaps—may come across as confident, their underlying insecurities and shame are unconscious. They adore social media because, although unaware, they are constantly looking for external approval. In just a few seconds, their demand for validation is satisfied.

Since they have spent years covering up and repressing all of their emotions, the uneasiness and shame are invisible. It is as though they have been taught to suppress their feelings. For the narcissist's partner, who needs emotional connection as their love language, this could be quite upsetting. A narcissist appears charming and charismatic on the outside. It's all a part of the façade to cover up their emotional dysregulation and other emotional difficulties on the inside. They are lively people who captivate the attention of others.

The nature of narcissism is nonlinear. We will study the four groups that comprise the seven different types of narcissists in the upcoming chapter. In order to recognize these characteristics in people who are closest to us or who aspire to be near us, it is imperative that we never stop studying and educating ourselves on this subject. When it comes to seeing others' vulnerability and taking advantage of it, narcissistic behaviors can be predatory. They are fiercely competitive and will do whatever it takes to put others down to succeed in business, the workplace, or any other aspect of life. We accomplish this as we delve deeply into the details so you may comprehend the kind of person who exhibits these qualities. Let's learn how to deal with these people and relationships so we don't allow them to hurt our emotions.

Chapter 2: The Development of Narcissistic Personality Disorder

There are a few possible causes for the disorder, much like with any mental illness or personality disorder. These factors may manifest separately or in combination in an individual's life, subsequently promoting a personality disorder's emergence and progression.

Genetics is the first missing piece in the genesis of NPD. It is quite probable that children and other relatives will experience NPD if a family member experiences the condition. Psychobiology, which holds that behavior and the brain are intertwined, is the reason behind this. A person is likely to inherit the genes that caused the brain's genetic wiring to occur in a way that results in NPD if their parents' and grandparents' genes left the brain wired in a particular way. Individuals with a genetic tendency are more likely than those without to experience NPD.

Parenting problems are another trigger for NPD. A person is more likely to develop NPD if they have parents or live in a family setting where they are overindulged, treated like royalty all the time, or given everything they ask for without realizing there are boundaries. Without boundaries and discipline, children will develop distorted ideas of who they are and how the world operates as they age. Their worldview encompasses the notion that they are unique and flawless.

However, NPD can also emerge in those who have extremely strict parents who don't respect their children's accomplishments. The youngster builds a defense system to counteract the unfavorable and persistent criticism they encounter. Imagine it as the opposite of a pendulum swinging. To counteract the negativity they are exposed to on a daily basis, children who experience excessive harshness from their parents may begin to overcompensate by thinking they are special, entitled to everything, and deserving of the world. Generally speaking, this is believed to occur when a youngster overcompensates to please their parent. Their goal is to win their parents' affection and respect.

Whatever kind of parent the person with NPD had, the child's early years—typically before the age of three—were when the parental behaviors started.

Society's notions about what and who is important are a third component that could be crucial to the development of NPD. For instance, the mainstream media's obsession with the wealthy, influential, and powerful has engendered the deeply held perception that these individuals are more significant than "ordinary people." Even watching reality TV idealizes those who are conceited, egotistical, and impolite to others while marginalizing or ignoring others who are kind and empathetic. Second, those who are more intelligent, wealthy, or of a higher standing are likelier to be well-liked by others. People could be motivated to strive for this higher position in order to get the same kind of recognition as a result. Lastly, our society is becoming less of a community. Youngsters struggle to identify with others since they are not frequently raised to feel they are a part of something greater than themselves. Their lofty self-image takes the place of their capacity for empathy.

However, the development of any personality disorder is typically the result of a combination of environmental variables, both personal and cultural, as well as genetic elements. If one or more parents or close relatives suffer from the disease, the child is likely to inherit the trait from their parents as well as grow up in an unstable home setting where it is more likely to manifest. It is simple to understand why the condition becomes so challenging to treat, given that many of the characteristics have been demonstrated to exist since childhood.

That does not, however, imply that those with NPD or their families have no options or treatments. The upcoming chapter will provide some hints regarding the current psychiatric and medical treatments for narcissistic personality disorder.

The diagram explaining the emergence of narcissistic tendencies and narcissistic personality disorder (NPD) can be found on the next page.

Chapter 5: Establishing Positive Connections

Developing Sincere Relationships

Developing real connections is a life-changing process that builds sincere, meaningful bonds marked by emotional closeness, understanding, and mutual trust. Fostering real connections in the context of overcoming narcissism necessitates a conscious transition from self-centeredbehavior to a more reciprocal and empathic attitude. The following are essential guidelines for developing sincere relationships in order to overcome narcissism:

Develop Self-Awareness:

A meaningful connection can only be nurtured by starting with self-awareness. Recognize the mental processes, feelings, and actions that are connected to narcissistic tendencies in yourself. This self-awareness establishes the groundwork for deliberate transformation.

Put humility into practice:

Recognize that everyone has both strengths and shortcomings in order to embrace humility. Give up the urge to always be the better person and instead recognize every individual's distinct traits and viewpoints to the partnership.

Be Sincere in Your Interest:

Inquire about the experiences, ideas, and emotions of others around you to show that you genuinely care about them. Create an atmosphere where others feel heard and appreciated by actively listening without bringing up yourself again.

Transmit Sincerity:

It takes an authentic self to foster true connections. Communicate honestly about your feelings, experiences, and weaknesses. By being open and honest, you inspire others to do the same, strengthening the bond between you on an emotional level.

Develop Empathy Constantly:

Bring empathy to all of your interactions. Make an effort to comprehend, without passing judgment, the feelings and viewpoints of others. Make sure your responses and actions are guided by empathy by checking in with yourself regularly.

Honor the Achievements of Others:

Develop an attitude of sincere gratitude for other people's accomplishments. Celebrate their accomplishments rather than feeling intimidated or jealous. This makes the relationship atmosphere positive and encouraging.

Stay in the Now:

Being completely present in the moment is necessary for fostering real connections. Reduce outside distractions and focus entirely on the person you are interacting with. Your presence demonstrates your respect for the other person and your importance in the partnership.

Exhibit Consistency:

Trust is developed via consistency. Try to maintain consistency between your words and deeds by keeping the values of reciprocity and empathy in check. The stability of real connections is influenced by predictability and dependability.

Offer your regrets and grow from them:
Acknowledge that you are not perfect and that everyone makes mistakes. When required, offer honest regrets and seize the chance to improve yourself. Acknowledging your errors reminds you of your dedication to developing sincere relationships.

Set Up Healthful Limits:
Respecting and setting appropriate limits is essential to fostering real connections. Be mindful of others' boundaries and express your own clearly and concisely. This fosters an atmosphere of emotional safety and trust.

Show Your Appreciation:
Give thanks regularly to people in your life for their presence and contributions. Being grateful creates a happy environment and shows how much you cherish and appreciate the relationship.

Put in the Time and Work:

Sincere relationships take time and work to develop. Deep talks, common experiences, and bond-building activities. This investment enhances the depth and durability of the relationship.

In conclusion, developing sincere relationships is a healing process that is consistent with conquering narcissism. It entails being self-aware, humble, showing genuine interest, sharing authentically, demonstrating ongoing empathy, celebrating the accomplishments of others, being present, being consistent, learning from mistakes, setting appropriate limits, expressing gratitude, and devoting time and energy. By emulating these ideals, people can cultivate relationships marked by emotional closeness, reciprocity, and authenticity.

Applying The Grey Rock Approach

Because we co-parent, are related to them as a mother-in-law, work with them, or have other obligations, we occasionally have to deal with narcissists and cannot choose never to talk to them again. Or, for example, because we are unable to stop the relationship immediately due to an impending divorce or house sale.

The Grey Rock Method will help you maintain your sanity when interacting with these poisonous people. Grey rocking is effective because narcissists always try to create drama and mayhem in order to elicit an emotional response from you. By using the Grey Rock Method, you prevent it from occurring.

You turn into a grey rock, uninteresting. I would say, "This is boring; it doesn't respond to me; it doesn't do anything," if I were holding a grey rock.

Removing your feelings from the situation means you are not providing the narcissist with the supply they sorely require.

Grey rocking begins with you giving up all information about your weaknesses, past trauma, and inner thoughts and emotions to the narcissist. Because narcissists thrive on dominance and power, they will stop at nothing to obtain the upper hand. They will use your vulnerabilities and any childhood trauma you may have shared with them as leverage against you.

In order to obtain what they want, they will tell you that you are insane this week if you tell them about a depressing emotion you had a week ago. So stop doing that now. Simply don't tell them anything else going forward if you have already given them personal information.

Never allow yourself to become emotional while you are stroking a narcissist. You refuse to fall for their bait when they trick you into doing it.

When your narcissistic mother-in-law acts passive-aggressively towards you, for instance, and says:

"Hey, how did the altercation at work with your boss? I know how difficult it is for you to get along with others.

Something impartial would be a grey rock response:

"Oh, that issue has been resolved, but thank you for your concern."

This is an example of a narcissist seeming to be concerned in order to poke fun at you and suggest that you are a challenging individual. You know exactly what she is doing, but you are not reacting emotionally externally—you are not becoming upset, you are not confronting her for being passive-aggressive, and you are not giving in to her demands.

When you engage in grey rocking, you should just use one word or sentence to communicate with the other person.

You can respond like this if they start bugging you about something from the past:

"I didn't see things that way." Alternatively, you may state, "That was your understanding of the situation."
"I am unable to discuss this at this time."

Or you could just say, "Okay," turn around, and go.

When you co-parent with a narcissist, you are limiting the conversations to the kids and making sure they never go outside of your boundaries.

It will have a voice similar to this:

"You have to come get our daughter on Wednesday at six o'clock."
"Please bring our son's lunchbox to school tomorrow; he left it at your house."

Consider grey rocking as you would speak with a Department of Motor Vehicles representative. As you enter, your goal is to leave as soon as possible. Simply provide the cashier with the necessary information, then go about your day. Saying, "I need to renew my license," you would provide the paperwork to the clerk and make your fast escape. Everything there is business-related and devoid of emotion.

Chapter 2: Handling Narcissistic Behaviour

Knowing when to spot a narcissist is only the first step. The next step is to learn how to move past the experiences and any fallout after realizing that you have one in your life. Being around a narcissist can be emotionally and mentally taxing. In order to reduce any potential bad repercussions, it is essential to deal with the situation appropriately as soon as possible.

Handling a Narcissist

Managing an egotistical person requires a great deal of practice. There is a learning curve since they are not like people who don't have narcissism, and dealing with this is not something you do with many people regularly. The most crucial thing is to never undervalue yourself in their eyes. They desire this, but there are ways to identify that and ensure you're setting and upholding appropriate boundaries.

Refrain from Fulfilling Their Fantasy

When interacting with a narcissist, it's critical to resist giving in to their delusion. It can be difficult to resist them because they can be so charming. Essentially, it doesn't take long to become entangled in their web. You may initially feel special and important to them, but this feeling passes quickly. Remember the following to avoid succumbing to the illusion:

They won't provide for your necessities. It's crucial to remember that you won't even be able to identify what you need or want. What you can do for them and what you can do to feed their ego is what a narcissist thinks makes you valuable.

Observe closely how they interact with others. It will be evident to you that they have no problem lying, manipulating, disrespecting, and harming other people. This conduct and manner of handling things will eventually catch up with you.

Removing the rose-colored glasses is necessary, even though it's not easy. You must assess how they treat you, even though it is not easy. Denial regarding someone's true nature is the easiest thing to do when you care about them, but you have to set this aside if you want to deal with a narcissist as effectively as possible.

Make sure your dreams don't slip your mind. It is simple to become engrossed in the illusions and fantasies of someone you are close to who is a narcissist. You must avoid losing yourself in this since doing so could make it difficult to regain control of who you are.

Define your boundaries and honor them.

Establishing and maintaining good boundaries is one of the most important components of a successful relationship. This can be difficult because, of course, a narcissist does not comprehend boundaries. Recall that mutual respect and consideration need to be the cornerstones of your relationships with other people. Even though you cannot provide what you receive, you must treat the relationship as your own. This will lessen the likelihood that someone will cross your bounds.

A narcissist, for instance, has no compunction about obtaining what they desire. You may have a narcissistic female friend who will just go through your wardrobe whenever she feels like it and steal anything. This friend would ask first in a typical friendship, but narcissists don't bother to ask for permission. They believe they are entitled to everything, even anything you may have that they might find appealing.

If you've been in a relationship with a narcissist for any length of time, you'll undoubtedly notice that they consistently disregard your boundaries. Create a plan to address this. What you intend to accomplish with it should serve as the foundation for your plan. Next, think about how you'll carry out the strategy and what will happen if the narcissist crosses your boundaries. The most crucial aspect of your strategy is that you resist caving into the narcissist's demands and maintain your resolve. Don't forget to inform them when someone crosses your boundaries.

Be ready for alterations in your relationships. Narcissists take offense when others fail to recognize them and bow to their every whim. They want you to support them and give them the last say in all decisions. They won't be thrilled that you are sticking up for yourself, so they will probably treat you differently once you start setting limits. They can try to humiliate or punish you, or they might take a different approach and trick you into returning to give in to their demands by acting charmingly.

You could set boundaries gently if you want to do everything you can to keep the friendship intact. For example, organize what you want to say and then present it clearly, collected, and courteously rather than suddenly changing things and explaining why you're doing it harshly. Just leave the conversation if it is not progressing as you had hoped. Refrain from engaging with the individual, allowing them to manipulate you into returning to your previous behavior, or simply caving into their demands.

Refrain from Taking Things Personally

Although it will be one of your hardest tasks, it is crucial. It is not the deliberate goal of a narcissist to harm you. They can't see anything wrong with their behavior because this is just who they are. Remember that their feelings, behaviors, and actions are not directed toward you. It's all about them in this.

A narcissist will make an effort to transform you into a person they can manipulate the most. So that their perception of you does not become how you see yourself, you must focus on your self-esteem and recognize your value. Don't let their negative affect how you feel about yourself; let them keep their negativity.

It follows that you must be aware of your identity. On the other hand, you must examine yourself honestly. You can easily leave a situation if a narcissist is targeting one of your strengths. You are aware of your proficiency at it. Do not let them diminish you; instead, take pride in it.

Avoid arguing with them. This will be difficult when your first reaction is to defend yourself when someone is attacking you. Keep in mind that a narcissist lacks rationality, and no amount of reasoning you apply to support your position can alter this. Just politely express your disagreement, then turn to leave.

Finally, never seek validation from a narcissist. Even if they may say kind things to you, their main goal is to dominate and manipulate you. You don't need their approval for everything you think or do as long as you believe in your values and have a strong sense of self-worth.

What Constitutes a Narcissist in Chapter 2?

In the early 1900s, Freud was the one who brought narcissism to the field of psychology. Psychologists have developed assessments to ascertain if an individual fits the definition of a narcissist. Research indicates that while many are female, narcissists tend to be men. In this book, the narcissist will be referred to as "he" a lot to keep things easy. But remember that we could be talking about a female as much as a male.

9 Characteristics of Narcissists

The nine characteristics listed below are dead giveaways for identifying a narcissist. This list is a terrific place to start, even though it isn't exhaustive.

Magnificence

Even though there is little proof to support his claims, the narcissist still hopes to be seen as superior.

obsession with achievement and power

They have delusions of grandeur, power, intelligence, beauty, and the perfect love.

Absence of compassion

They lack the ability or willingness to understand or relate to the needs or feelings of others.

conceited and overbearing

They want to be in charge and feel better than other people.

Overindulgence in admiration

They hate it when others are in the spotlight because they desire attention.

Taking advantage of other people

They don't hesitate to exploit and rob people of their life. Their primary concern is taking as much as they can from other people.

The Conviction that one is special

They believe only those who share their uniqueness and special qualities can relate to or understand them.

Possessing an entitlement complex

They think that others owe them favors and have irrational expectations of them. They have no appreciation for what people do for them.

Being jealous of other people

They are bitter when others get what they want because they feel entitled. They also frequently believe that other people are jealous of them.

Some well-known personalities may immediately spring to mind after reading these traits: Scarlett O'Hara from Gone with the Wind, Dorian from The Picture of Dorian Grey, Tony Stark from Ironman, Miranda Priestly (played by Meryl Streep), Lucy from Charlie Brown, and many more.

NPD vs. narcissistic

The American Psychology Association first recognized narcissistic personality disorder, or

NPD, in 1980. Narcissistic characteristics are not always associated with NPD. There are several levels of narcissism. An individual with NPD is defined as having at least five of the characteristics above.

Narcissists are more obvious due to their blatantly irritating behavior. On the other hand, deceitful and cunning people with NPD are more common. They con others into thinking they are endearing and admirable role models for society. Their "Echoes," or those closest to them, are the only ones to whom they reveal their real, evil selves. Their narcissistic tendencies are ingrained in them, and they take great care to maintain their image. They will remain a secret until they have earned your love and trust.

Surprisingly, people can genuinely think that their front is genuine. They have unrealistic expectations for their abilities and accomplishments. They have such a high opinion of themselves that they take offense at criticism personally. They have no actual pals and have no regrets about mistreating others. As long as they stand to benefit, they find nothing wrong with ruining the reputations of others.

NPD sufferers believe they are superior to everyone else and consider themselves to be gods. He constantly needs attention and needs his ego to be constantly stimulated. He believes he has the right to punish the wayward subject if his requirements are not satisfied. He almost seems like a sociopath. It is said that while not all sociopaths are narcissists, all narcissists are sociopaths.

Sensitivity And Narcissism: An Unspoken Paradox

I inquire, "Have you ever seen an iceberg?" realizing that not many people have had the opportunity to witness one up close. However, everyone is aware of the iceberg metaphor. Ninety percent of its mass is hidden from view beneath the water's surface. A mystery that is concealed. You see, reader, narcissism is like an iceberg. Only a small portion of reality is revealed to us on the outside. There is a depth of feelings and sensitivities beneath that exterior layer of haughtiness and self-obsession. I'd like to invite you to plunge into this chasm and examine the dichotomy between sensitivity and narcissism in this section of the journey.

Sensitivity is frequently linked to compassion, empathy, and the capacity to recognize subtle emotional cues. In contrast, narcissism is frequently linked to a lack of empathy, an obsessive focus on oneself, and a detachment from other people. So, how is it possible for a person to embody both of these seemingly incompatible ideas? This query gets to the core of what psychologists refer to as "covert" or "vulnerable" narcissism.

In his paper "Narcissism and the Self: A Reevaluation" (2018), psychologist and University of Georgia psychology professor Joshua D. Miller defines *vulnerable narcissism* as a type of narcissism marked by insecurity, hypersensitivity, and defensiveness. Vulnerable narcissism can be less obvious and frequently presents as extreme sensitivity, in contrast to grandiose narcissism, which is more obvious and marked by overwhelming self-confidence.

Naturally, this sensitivity is a hypersensitivity to one's wants, feelings, and perceptions rather than a genuine sensitivity to others. A person who exhibits susceptible narcissism may be very vulnerable to rejection, criticism, and any other perceived danger to their sense of self-worth. But is this merely another manifestation of self-obsession, or is it true sensitivity?

We must distinguish between the two, much like a detective investigating a crime scene. A highly sensitive person exhibits sensitivity to herself, others, and the outside world. It is the capacity to tune into life's emotional nuances and complexity, as well as an openness to new experiences. It is not a means of self-defense or ego protection.

Do you recall from Chapter 2 our discussion of how our mental mirror might skew how we see ourselves? We are now investigating how that distortion can show up as misguided sensitivity, which is more concerned with defending our ego than actually relating to others.

I encourage you to consider your personal experiences as we continue this trip. Have you come across a vulnerable narcissist who matches this description? Have you personally engaged in these actions and felt these emotions? How might you distinguish between oversensitivity driven by ego and genuine sensitivity? Your response to these questions may reveal previously undiscovered facets of your character or aid in your understanding of others around you. As Socrates, the philosopher, once observed, "Life without examination is not worth living." Therefore, I'm asking you to investigate, consider, and go into the murky and deep waters of sensitivity and narcissism.

But first, consider why this knowledge is important. Why is it important that we comprehend the conflict between sensitivity and narcissism? Like any journey, the key to enjoying it is knowing why each step is done the way it is.

Consider yourself an adventurer embarking on a journey to uncharted territory. Your goal is not just to get where you're going; it's also to comprehend and absorb the environment around you. Gaining insight into the intricacies of narcissism and sensitivity can help you better navigate relationships, control your emotions, and perhaps even assist others on their path of self-discovery. Thus, dear reader, never undervalue the importance of knowledge. A renowned scientist, Carl Sagan, famously stated, "We are a way for the cosmos to know itself."

Now that the why has been established, we may explore the what in more detail. What precisely do we need to comprehend the dichotomy of sentience and narcissism?

In his book "The Big Five Personality Traits" (2019), psychology professor Oliver John of the University of California, Berkeley, explores the complex realm of human personality and emphasizes how particular personality qualities can interact in nuanced and perhaps contradictory ways. John asserts that although sensitivity and narcissism seem to be mutually exclusive, they are frequently inextricably linked. According to his studies, narcissism has a good correlation with extraversion and openness to new experiences. However, it can also be linked to excessive entitlement and heightened sensitivity to rejection and criticism.

Isn't it interesting how a single personality may have two seemingly incompatible traits? It resembles a maelstrom of behaviors and feelings that converge and diverge, giving rise to a fascinatingly complex personality.

Consider someone you know who seems to radiate confidence and authority and possesses a strong sense of self. Imagine the same individual now losing it at the first sign of rejection or criticism. Although it might appear contradictory, this illustrates the intricacy of the human soul.

You might be wondering, at this point, how we handle this. How do we make our way through this maze of paradoxes and complexities? We must delve even further into the connection between narcissism and sensitivity in order to provide answers to these queries. We must comprehend how these two aspects intersect and how they may materialize in our day-to-day existence.

Any competent explorer knows that traveling is more than merely seeing and documenting. It also involves communication, involvement, and engagement. I invite you to continue on this adventure, dear reader. I cordially welcome you to delve further into the enigma surrounding narcissism and sensitivity, to get fresh perspectives, and to recognize your place in this complex dance of the human psyche.

Are you prepared to carry on with the voyage now? Are you prepared to descend even further into sensitivity and narcissism? It may be a difficult trip, but a deeper comprehension of yourself and others. And that's a precious gift, my dear reader.

Allow me to tell you a tale to help you understand this concept. Consider Mariana as a lady. Mariana is a prominent corporate leader renowned for her fortitude and decisiveness. She is the picture of confidence in the eyes of the people. Behind the scenes, though, Mariana battles low self-esteem. She fears failing and disappointing both herself and other people. She is extremely sensitive to rejection and criticism; even the smallest criticism can break her.

Despite her prosperous work and outward confidence, Mariana feels like an imposter, always worried that people will find out who the "real her" is. Mariana is extremely sensitive and shields herself from the outside world with an armor of confidence despite her seeming narcissism.

This is but one instance of how the dichotomy between sensitivity and narcissism might appear in the actual world. But how are we going to get across this contradictory sea?

Authenticity is a crucial component of personal development, as American psychologist Carl Rogers noted in his 1961 book "On Becoming a Person." Rogers asserts that we must develop the ability to accept and value every aspect of who we are, including the seemingly contradictory ones.

Consider a piece of paper. You have sensitivity on the one hand and narcissism on the other. You have to learn how to fold the paper so that both sides may coexist instead of attempting to erase one or the other. It's important to recognize how one side enhances the other rather than trying to eliminate them.

You cannot have one without the other, much like a coin with two sides. Strength cannot exist without weakness, and confidence cannot exist without vulnerability. You must learn to view these characteristics as two sides of the same coin rather than opposites.

I thus urge you, my dear reader, to see past outward manifestations. I want you to acknowledge the richness and complexity of your individuality. I want you to accept and value your sensitivity as much as your selfishness. All of these characteristics ultimately contribute to what makes you special and human.

Are you up to overcoming labels to uncover your genuine self and explore beyond them? Because, as you always remember, each step you take on this journey puts you one step closer to who you are, and that is a very worthwhile journey, my dear reader.

You can run into difficulties on your path of self-discovery. You will experience uncertainties and anxieties and may question your ability to truly make a change. However, I want you to know that you are traveling with others.

You, too, can overcome your anxieties and obstacles, just as Mariana did. All it takes is the guts to face what you see when you glance into your reflection. Do you think you can rise to the challenge?

In his seminal work "Emotional Intelligence" (1995), Dr. Daniel Goleman contends that empathy and introspection are essential to emotional intelligence. This implies that you are raising your emotional intelligence as well as your level of self-awareness. You can better understand and relate to people by acknowledging and appreciating your sensitivity. You are enhancing your sense of self-efficacy and your capacity to affect your surroundings by accepting your narcissism.

This is ultimately a voyage of personal development. A voyage of self-discovery and interpersonal comprehension. A journey that will enable you to see the genuine nature of humanity and help you get beyond labels and preconceptions.

However, the adventure doesn't end here. In the upcoming chapter, we shall examine how assertiveness affects how one perceives oneself. You'll learn how assertiveness may be useful in your self-discovery journey and how it desires.

I now extend an invitation to proceed, dear reader. I'm asking you to be open to new possibilities and to open your heart and intellect. Because, as you always remember, this is your path, and every step you take will bring you one step closer to honesty and emotional fulfillment. Are you prepared to find out what is ahead in the upcoming chapter? I promise that you will learn priceless lessons and obtain insightful knowledge. Come on, the journey has only just started.

Chapter 3: Healing from Narcissistic Abuse

Move On

There are going to be several challenging times in a relationship with a narcissist. There will be moments when you want to quit because you feel so mistreated, ashamed, and alone. You'll experience fatigue, worthlessness, and rejection. Even though you will be in excruciating pain, you will try to convince yourself that everything is fine in order to feel better because you do not want to confront the truth of the situation. But once you realize you were just fooling yourself, you will eventually feel worse. There will be moments when you'll feel trapped in a jail with no way out. It will be a difficult process, but you have to start somewhere. To begin with, educate yourself to be resistant to their egotism. Here's how to accomplish it.

Live your life as you see fit, with independence and determination.

Don't let conversations and disagreements sap your feelings and vitality.

Refrain from praising, noticing, and complimenting the person—these things bolster the narcissist.

Don't talk for too long with the person. Narcissists take pleasure in being the center of attention, and you are giving them energy when you interact with them.

Refrain from comparing yourself to the narcissist. Even though you want to give them a taste of their medicine because they are bothering you, this is not a smart idea. You will ultimately lose because the narcissist will take pleasure in arguing back and forth with you.

Recall that you are not an experienced player; the narcissist is.

The narcissist in your life will eventually grow tired of you. They only stay when they have something to gain, and they will look elsewhere since you are no longer giving them a narcissistic supply because their actions and remarks don't affect you. You can be sure your name will be dragged through the mud once they discover another victim. To make their next victim feel sorry for them, they will tell their new partner how awful you were and how poorly you treated them.

After they've left, you'll experience a time of mourning during which you'll begin to feel sorry for the narcissist. You'll persuade yourself that their extreme depression is the only reason they are acting this way. Feeling this way is unnecessary because everything in the narcissist's actions and words is deliberate and well-planned. They don't do random actions or behave in desperation. They are highly skilled at what they do. Since narcissist only experiences depression when their supply runs out, they will search for fresh stimuli elsewhere (alcohol, drugs, the other sex, shopping, etc.). They return to their regular selves once they have their supplies. To help you overcome your guilt trip, try doing the following instead of sitting around feeling sorry for yourself.

Exercise, eat healthfully, and take good care of your physical body.

Take a stroll and spend time with folks who will lift your spirits.

To get it out of your system, speak with trustworthy individuals.

For as long as you need to, cry and scream.

Take a lengthy bath or shower to unwind.

Rent a movie or go to the movies; this will help you forget your problems.

Get in the habit of journaling; it will assist you in identifying and releasing negative feelings.

Invest in something lovely for yourself.

Volunteering will demonstrate that taking care of others comes before your egotistical spouse.

Engage in complementary therapies like the Emotional Freedom Technique. These are useful treatments that help people let go of and get past difficult emotions.

Embrace the company of upbeat individuals who inspire you to believe there is hope for the future.

Anything in your home that makes you think of your relationship should be removed.

Give that clothing to a good cause and start dressing the way you want to if your controlling partner only lets you wear what they prefer.

You should now focus on taking care of yourself instead of your narcissistic partner.

The next thing you should do, now that you are aware that you are dealing with a narcissist is to avoid them at all costs. This is the challenging portion! As you've read, extreme narcissists are completely devoid of empathy. Within a few weeks of being in their presence, they make everyone around them feel awful. It is very doubtful that they are even slightly conscious of how they are acting and much less likely that they will look in the mirror and decide to change.

You will be tempted to want to correct the narcissist's mistakes since you are a normal person with feelings and real compassion for other people, but this is not a smart idea. It will backfire on you; they'll become more defensive, and they could even be able to persuade you that you are the one who is having issues. You will never get a fair bargain from an extreme narcissist, and if you stay in their presence, your life will continue to be unpleasant.

You'll have to decide, and you'll have to decide quickly. While ending a connection is never easy, it will usually be the simplest with romantic partners, coworkers, friends, and, in certain situations, family members. You are typically not legally required to continue your friendship with these individuals. For instance, there is no dependant involved, you do not jointly own a piece of real estate, you do not jointly operate a business, and no will administration is occurring. Getting out of a relationship like this is possible once these conditions do not bind you. You may truly care about the other person, so this may be a tough decision, but no one should continue in a relationship that is emotionally harming them. Shutting all windows, doors, and mailboxes entails breaking all contact. Don't allow them to contact you by chat, text, or email, and block them on all social networking sites. Should there be any space left unfilled, they will use every effort to regain your favor. Avoid listening to voicemails or reading previous texts. You can fall into their trap by feeling sorry for them when you hear them crying and pleading. Everything they say to you after you cut them off will come from a place of manipulation and rage, which is not helpful for the healing process.

You don't want to constantly think about this individual, even if you will never fully forget about them. As such, requesting that friends and family refrain from discussing the individual or inquiring whether you have heard from them is a good idea. Additionally, you ought to request that they withhold any information on you. Because narcissists are so endearing, everyone finds them to be endearing, which makes them dangerous. Likely, your loved ones won't comprehend your decision to call it quits on the partnership. He will likely be well-liked by your friends and family and will take advantage of this to re-establish communication. "Please give me her number; I just want to talk; I just want to understand what I have done wrong so I can fix it," he will sob as he arrives at your parents' house, claiming he doesn't understand why you have treated him this way. Your loved ones must be firm and tell him they will not be giving him their contact details.

You must limit your alone time during the early phases of the breakup. You're going to feel lonely at first. You and this person were presumably in a relationship for a while, but now you are alone. Second, spending too much time alone will cause you to reflect and question whether you made the proper decision. In order to avoid going back, it is crucial that you stay as distracted as possible throughout this period.

Spend no time blaming yourself or thinking that there was something you could have done to make things different. Regretfully, you are not unfamiliar with this mode of thought. Narcissistic abuse victims are led to believe that they are to blame for all that occurs to them. They invest much time and effort into figuring out what went wrong or what they could have done differently to start this. Please realize that you have no power to alter a narcissist; it is impossible. All they can do is transform themselves. You should concentrate on changing yourself because you are the only one you can truly alter. You should be thinking along these lines: "Now that your awful and unhealthy relationship is over, you need to concentrate on getting well on your own."

The hurt that comes from realizing your ex-partner was never truly in love with you is another feeling you'll have to cope with. Love is not bad; it doesn't bring about suffering. After coming to this understanding, you will feel unlovable, which is incredibly tough to handle.

You'll wonder if you deserved to be handled this way. Even though it aches, it is a waste of time and energy to think this way. You have to consider the facts: By your standards, you should never have been treated in this manner, regardless of how someone defines love or whether they can express it. Someone with a personality problem cannot love anyone, not themselves. Thus, you will never discover true love with them.

Change how you think about yourself when you question whether your spouse truly loves you. Remind yourself that you are valuable and deserving of love and that there are individuals who will show you unconditional love and won't take advantage of your mental and emotional vulnerabilities.

Professional Careers and Pathological Narcissism: The Ascent and Triumph of the Narcissist

The variety of traits that comprise the narcissistic personality type has been demonstrated. These characteristics together can have a big impact on how the narcissist behaves at work, which can help them advance quickly and seem to be successful in their career. Despite their horrible and destructive personalities, it may seem inconceivable that these people are where they are. Nevertheless, let's examine the effects of pathological narcissism on a person's profession and the potential long-term consequences.

Charm and Quick Career Advancement: Pathological narcissists frequently possess charm and are adept at leaving a lasting impression on others. They have the charisma and confidence to readily influence superiors and coworkers. Since they are seen as strong and competent leaders, this might result in a quick ascent up the corporate ladder.

An excessive amount of ambition and competitiveness characterizes pathological narcissists. They'll stop at nothing to accomplish their objectives and win respect. This motivation forces them to always look for fresh chances for development, which propels them to assume more visible and responsible responsibilities in their professions.

Situational Flexibility: Psychological narcissists typically exhibit a high degree of flexibility in responding to a variety of environments and people. Blending in with the business environment and coming across as "the right person at the right time" might help someone succeed professionally and build their reputation.

Pathological narcissists are experts at promoting themselves and projecting a powerful professional image. They will make a concerted effort to establish a solid reputation for success and highlight their accomplishments to set themselves up for future career advancement.

Incapacity to Take Criticism and Failures: Although pathological narcissism can produce early success, narcissists frequently find it difficult to take criticism and setbacks. When someone criticizes them, they could respond too sensitively, getting defensive or even hostile. Interpersonal relationships and one's long-term professional reputation may suffer due to such behavior.

Manipulation and Destructive Competition: In an effort to outwit and acquire what they want, pathological narcissists may use manipulative strategies. This conduct can weaken team cohesiveness and collaboration and create a toxic work atmosphere.

Potentially Negative Long-Term Effects: Pathological narcissists may experience difficulties in their jobs down the road, even if they have early success. Once people discover their genuine motivations, damaged interpersonal relationships, a lack of empathy, and a propensity to sacrifice others' well-being for personal gain can all contribute to a deterioration in one's career. This implies that you won't have to put up with them indefinitely.

In conclusion, pathological narcissism frequently has its own set of weaknesses and limitations, even though it may offer a speedy route to success. Comprehending the working dynamics of these personalities can assist individuals and organizations in managing their possible effects and making well-informed choices on their interactions and approaches to management.

Comprehending And Getting Past Grief

After experiencing narcissistic abuse, you are left with two intense feelings inside of you: sadness and rage. Remember that each of these feelings has a proper place for a full recovery. These are very normal responses to any kind of distressing event. In this chapter, we'll discuss what grief is and how it fits into the healing process. Anger is the other emotion; we shall address it in a different chapter.

Lamenting the Absence of Your Mother

Being the daughter of a narcissistic mother means that one of the things you have to get over is grieving for the things you never had as a child—things like love, support, and real connections.

Because your narcissistic mother always had something else in mind when she laughed with you, you never really shared true laughter with her. There was always an underlying reason. She never truly became sensitive to you.

You can feel it when you're grieving. It facilitates your release from the labels that were placed on you. Additionally, it might assist you in letting go of the crippling worry that perhaps no one will ever love you.

Permit yourself to cry for the mother you never had and deserved. Some claim that venting your fury by yelling, screaming, or slamming the bed and pillows doesn't make you feel better. Indeed, using those aggressive methods to express anger won't make it go away.

However—and there's a major but—completing everything enables you to reconnect with your emotions. You come to understand that you are a unique person and not only your narcissistic mother's tool or extension. You grieve for something entirely for you, and you can feel yourself getting upset, proving that you are your own person.

The Grieving Process

Adult offspring of narcissistic moms experience five distinct stages of bereavement, which have been recognized and defined by research.

It's not necessary to go through these phases in a specific order. As one progresses through them, certain phases cross over with others. In the conversation that follows, let's examine each of these five phases:

• Gratitude

Acceptance is one stage in a grieving daughter's journey. She comes to terms with the fact that her egotistical mother didn't love her all that much. She also comes to terms with the fact that her mother was not particularly empathetic.

She also discovers that she can no longer live a life of denial. She regains the ability to address her emotions through acceptance. After realizing and acknowledging that there is a problem in their relationship with their narcissistic mother, individuals go on to the next phase of the rehabilitation process, which is acceptance.

• Despondency

A daughter will eventually experience some degree of depression when she comes to terms with the truth that she and her mother were never truly in love. The reality hits you hard.

She is very depressed. On the one hand, she has come to terms with the fact that she will never again have the love relationship she envisioned with her mother. Recall that a narcissistic mother's influence is greater on a daughter than on a boy.

She should have been the daughter's ideal role model, which is why she strongly influenced the daughter. Eventually, the daughter will come to terms with the fact that her mother will never be as loving as she once believed.

She'll watch the ties between her friends and their mothers and realize the affection she never had. She'll be envious of what she'll never have. Even though she lives in a house with her parents, she will practically feel like an orphaned girl.

She is going to let go of all those demands. She'll experience the start of depression. In keeping with it, she'll start to experience grief and rage as well.

• Haggling

Throughout her life, the daughter of a narcissistic mother has had to bargain for her mother's love and attention. They bargain both with her mother and among themselves. She will talk to herself in a very familiar way on the inside.

She will use various negotiating techniques, such as getting high grades, acting courteously, being kind, being obedient, and others, to declare, "If only I can become good enough, then my mom would love me."

She will eventually speak with her mother and try to negotiate with her. She'll volunteer to do one thing, hoping to negotiate a trip out for ice cream or something like that. While it does work occasionally, Mother simply won't bother or doesn't want to bother with her daughter most of the time.

As she compares what she's been experiencing with what she observes in other children, reality frequently becomes hazy during all this. A daughter may occasionally engage in internal bargaining even after she and her narcissistic mother have split up in order to reject the truth that she is now attempting to deal with.

This was the phase of the grieving process that I was in for a long time. I firmly believed that things would improve between my mother and myself if I changed and improved. Perhaps, I reasoned, I might persuade her that what she was doing was improper. It is possible; the issue is that I overinvested in attempting to make it work. My mother didn't even pledge to attempt to improve; I did all the work.

I was lucky that my brother acted as a reality check for me and made me realize that no matter how much I bargained, it wouldn't get me our mother's love. Even after I consciously realized it wouldn't work and moved in with my brother, I kept telling myself, "Maybe if I just make an effort to reach out first, she'll be touched enough to compromise."

- Anger

Anger is a different phase of the grief process. Unbelievably, taking this step is essential to getting over everything. Because her mother failed to meet her emotional needs, her daughter will be angry with her.

She will become irate because nothing less than the truth will let her lose all faith that her mother will change. Anger would be directed at the parent for all the bad things she has done and at oneself for letting things go to that extent.

Anger is a stage of feeling trapped. But no matter what you do, nothing will appease your fury, and you will continue to strike out at the world. How do you move past it? In the upcoming chapter, we will discuss that.

• Refusal

The little girl has lied to herself and others about the facts since she was a little toddler. She disputes some things that she knew all along, such as the fact that her mother doesn't truly love her and that her mother is incapable of empathetic behavior.

Why do narcissistic mothers' kids lie about what happened? They act in this way to stay alive. The youngster yearns for love above all else that she has received or will ever get. Even in the face of cognitive dissonance, she continues to deny the truth to grow.

Chapter 5: The Durability of Narcissistic Partnerships

For individuals who have endured abuse in a narcissistic, abusive relationship, understanding narcissism can be powerful. Because of this, narcissistic relationships seldom last. As you get to know a narcissist, you'll discover that they typically have trouble sustaining solid, enduring connections and partnerships. People often retain their distance or cut off communication entirely from narcissists once they become apparent to them. It's hard to keep a relationship going with their shallow feelings and lack of genuine connection and bonding.

Is it the narcissist's fault? Should the partner leave if the narcissist was handed the cards and it's not their fault? Yes, and a narcissist will always be a snake is the answer. Narcissists have poisonous characteristics. Whether they acknowledge it or not, the narcissist will ultimately cause harm to people in their vicinity.

The victim of a narcissistic relationship is usually advised to end things amicably. The drawback of this advice is that some people may find it impractical. It could be challenging for the victim to leave if they have financial obligations or children. Many victims are unable to simply leave the town. The victim may find it difficult to run into their abuser at work, at stores, or in other public settings.

It's difficult to leave a poisonous relationship with a wounded heart and a racing mind. Saying "no" to a loved one requires a great deal of bravery and strength of character. It takes time and help to find the strength to walk out.

A narcissist, particularly a poisonous one, is vengeful. Until they are ready, they do not want to let go of their victims. To get their victim back, the narcissist will employ a variety of deceptive strategies. The narcissist will try to ruin them if that doesn't succeed.

Never announce your departure from a narcissistic partner to the victim. Should the narcissist be aware of the victims' plans, they will make every effort to thwart them. Hoovering is one tactic the narcissist employs. When a narcissist attempts to suck their victims back like a hoover, it's called hoovering. Even if the victim's partner may say they are sorry for what they did, the apology is not real. They might pledge to behave differently going forward.

When preparing to flee, the first thing a victim should do is confirm their financial stability. According to the National Collation Against Domestic Violence, financial hardships force almost 85% of women to re-enter violent relationships. The best course of action for someone to avoid this is to open a different bank account. A different P.O. box and email address are necessary for the victim in order to prevent the abuser from learning about the bank account. Additionally, it's a good idea to make sure that their abusive partner cannot just figure out the answers to all of the security questions. Some victims hold off on leaving until they receive a raise at work or receive their income taxes.

A victim may occasionally be financially entirely dependent on the abuser. The abuser may undermine the victims' efforts to obtain employment or independence. The internet offers a variety of side occupations that one could perform in their spare time. Most of these occupations pay via PayPal, which might be more discreet than opening a new bank account in the eyes of a spouse. Another choice would be to look for a shelter or victim advocacy agency if the victim cannot acquire financial aid and must leave. These locations can assist victims in obtaining financial assistance.

The individual leaving the victim should get in touch with a lawyer or shelter advocate as soon as possible if the victim has children. In order to prevent the abuser from reporting the children as abducted when you depart with them, it is crucial to inform others. Inform daycarecenters, schools, and other organizations of the situation. By keeping everyone informed, you can stop the abuser from visiting and taking the kids away.

Seek assistance outside of the narcissist's social group. The narcissist has already become part of the victim's social circle by the time their partner is prepared to depart. The narcissist has won over friends and relatives. They cast aside those they were unable to convince. If possible, the victim should begin attempting to mend some of the damaged connections in their life; they may feel guilty for allowing the relationships to go in the wrong path. The sufferer could be afraid of being rejected. For example, returning to the parents who may have inspired them could be challenging.

An excellent place to start for a victim who feels helpless is a victim advocate organization. A victim can contact the police or a doctor if they are unsure where to look for one. Getting help from a qualified therapist is also advised. A friend or family member may not be fully aware of the abuse the victim has experienced, but a therapist can assist them in overcoming emotional trauma.

Someone quitting an abusive relationship must tell their tale first. If the victim interacts with these individuals daily, for example, at work or in social situations, then telling the tale will be even more crucial. Proactively exposing the truth first will prevent or at least lessen any harm that a narcissist may have caused.

Children who witness a narcissistic breakup frequently find themselves used as puppets in a conflict. The victim should anticipate a protracted custody dispute with the narcissist. The child is no longer more than a trophy, regardless of how the narcissist perceives them.

The victim should select an experienced attorney after ending the relationship. The attorney ought to be somewhat knowledgeable about narcissistic personality disorder; the attorney might have handled divorce cases involving narcissistic parents in the past. It's acceptable to shop around until the victim locates a representative they feel at ease with.

The narcissist will attempt to elicit an emotional response from the victim in court in order to assert that they are unstable. When in public, the victim should try to maintain composure so as not to let the narcissist affect them.

Keep a record of everything. Text and email manipulation is simple. The victim must preserve any written correspondence they receive because of this. Should the narcissist have used physical aggression, the victim ought to document any injuries with photos.

When it comes to getting a divorce, the victim should have a strategy and follow it. What they wish to keep should be known by the victim. It should already be clear to them whether they desire exclusive custody or to co-parent. The narcissist is willing to fight for everything and will celebrate any small accomplishment.

The victim ought to be aware of their rights and have established limits. It is not required of the victims to allow the narcissist to see the kids whenever they please. The other parent should be allowed to visit on designated days.

You must give up blaming yourself for being in or out of a narcissistic relationship. Acknowledge that this individual is so skilled at manipulating other people's feelings for their gain that you were tricked into staying after their narcissistic qualities became apparent. Reiterate the belief that you are aware of better; you deserve better than their callous behavior. You may now see through their deception to your life's purpose because you know their true nature.

Chapter 2: Disorder of the Narcissistic Personality (NPD)

It is not always the case that someone with narcissistic tendencies has a personality disorder. The topic of personality disorders—more especially, narcissistic personality disorder (NPD)—will be covered in this chapter. We will examine the definition of NPD, its causes, the symptoms, signs, and indicators of an NPD sufferer, the diagnostic standards for NPD, and NPD treatments. This is a crucial chapter for you to read if you think you may be a victim of a narcissist in your life. It will explain why narcissists behave the way they do and offer some therapeutic options. Recall that NPD is a curable condition; therefore, if you are at ease with it, you may aid in the recovery of the narcissists in your life.

Recognising NPD

Because the term "narcissism" is so widely used in today's culture, it's common to misapply it to someone who exudes cockiness or excessive confidence. However, narcissism does not imply self-love when it comes to psychological terminology. It would be more realistic to say that people with NPD are infatuated and fixated on an elaborate and idealized version of themselves. Because it helps them conceal and avoid their uneasiness and low self-esteem, they adore their own abnormally inflated sense of self. But maintaining this delusional self-image takes a lot of work, which is where their dysfunctional attitudes and behaviors enter the picture.

In reality, NPD is composed of patterns that mimic conceited conduct and haughty thoughts. It also involves an overabundance of adoration and a lack of empathy. Individuals with NPD are frequently characterized as boastful, manipulative, demanding, condescending, and selfish. A narcissist's behavior and thought patterns are prevalent in all spheres of their life, including friendships, romantic relationships, family, and the workplace. Even when they are aware of their behavior, people with NPD are very reluctant to alter it; it is in their nature to place the blame elsewhere. As they are highly sensitive individuals, they will take offense at even the slightest disagreement or criticism because they see it as an attack on their person. To escape their anger or coldness, people in a narcissist's life find it easier to just comply with whatever demands they make. But as you get more knowledge about NPD, you'll be able to recognize the narcissists in your life, guard against their deception, and establish appropriate boundaries. In order for you to start recognizing narcissistic individuals in your life, let's examine the telltale signs and symptoms of this personality type.

NPD Symptoms And Signs

Determining who those individuals in your life are and taking appropriate precautions against them is perhaps the most crucial step in overcoming and recovering from narcissistic abuse. But before you can defend yourself, you need to identify the people in your life who are acting narcissistically. Let's examine the signs and symptoms:

Extreme self-importance-related emotions and beliefs

As we previously discovered, grandiosity is what distinguishes narcissism. More than just your typical conceit or haughtiness, grandiosity is an inflated sense of superiority. Individuals with non-psychotic personality disorder (NPD) frequently feel that they are too good for regular or normal things and that only other "special" people can truly understand them. They are only interested in connecting to high-status objects, individuals, or locations. In addition, narcissists think they are superior to others and demand respect for this, even when they have done nothing to merit it. They frequently embellish and lie about their skills and accomplishments. Furthermore, people only hear about their contributions, how wonderful they are, and how fortunate they are to have the chance to work with and get to know them when they discuss their relationships or professional endeavors. They constantly see themselves as the unquestioned star, and no one is nearly as special as them.

Always in need of praise from others.

A narcissist's belief of superiority is comparable to a balloon that is deflating and requires constant affirmation and appreciation to stay inflated. In their daily lives, an occasional complement is insufficient. Because narcissists require continual reinforcement for their inflated sense of self-worth, they gravitate toward others who will satiate their need for validation. These connections are frequently one-sided. It will never be the other way around; the focus of the connection is always on what the admirer can do to help the narcissist. The narcissist would consider it a betrayal if the admirer stopped or reduced their attention towards them.

severe delusions

Owing to their own self-deception and magical thinking, narcissists live in a warped universe where reality does not support their grandiose self-perception. Their self-glorifying illusions of unending success, beauty, power, intelligence, and perfect love give them a sense of control and uniqueness. Any information or facts that contradict their imaginations are either ignored or rationalized away to defend themselves against their inner feelings of emptiness and guilt. They respond to anything that can shatter their fantasy bubble by becoming extremely defensive and occasionally even aggressive. People who spend time with narcissists eventually learn to avoid their rejection of reality.

excessive entitlement

Narcissists demand special treatment from others because they believe they are unique. They think they can have anything they desire. Obediently comply with all of their whims. You are a useless person if you are not anticipating and satisfying the narcissist's every need. They would probably act out violently, become angry, or give you the cold shoulder if you dare to refuse their requests or ask them to do something for you in return.

persistently harassing other people

When they encounter someone who seems to have something they don't, narcissists frequently feel threatened, especially by people who come across as confident and well-liked. People who challenge them and won't bow to their requests also make them feel frightened. Disapproval is their automatic defense mechanism. Putting those folks down is the only way to remove the threat and restore some vigor to their injured ego. They could act dismissively or condescendingly to convey how little they value them to the other person. To get this person back in line, they might even go so far as to threaten, name-call, harass, and abuse them.

Taking advantage of people who are experiencing intense remorse or shame

As discussed in the first chapter, the characteristic that most distinguishes a narcissist is their lack of empathy. Stated differently, they never acquired the capacity to perceive and experience the emotions and sentiments of others. They see the people in their lives as tools to fulfill their demands. Because of this, they will readily exploit others to further their objectives. They may not realize that their exploitation of personal connections is frequently malevolent. Narcissists genuinely feel that other people are there to assist them in achieving their needs. Thus, they don't consider how their actions and behavior may affect other people. It would be impossible for a narcissist to comprehend this if you tried to convey it to them. They are only able to comprehend how to take care of themselves.

How To Coexist With An Idiostrophic

It cannot be overstated: cohabiting with a narcissist can be extremely difficult. It's a lot of labor, stress, and sadness to live with one.

Living with an individual who suffers from narcissistic personality disorder might be motivated by several factors such as love, having children and a marriage, or cultural or religious beliefs. In any case, the person supporting the person with NPD must make every effort to ensure the success of their relationship.

Most people eventually turn to psychological assistance to try to improve a relationship as much as possible. In case you are associated with someone who has NPD, please read this line once again. The key phrase here is "as good as possible." The best outcome will be a relationship that is as good as possible unless the narcissist is willing to participate in any kind of therapy to address their narcissistic disorder and how it is affecting you, family members, friends, and even coworkers.

This is about the basic knowledge one needs to deal with a partner who has narcissistic personality disorder. At the same time, they don't want to leave until they've tried everything to make it work in a relationship with them.

Knowing these three things will make your relationship with a narcissist run much more smoothly:

What coexisting with a narcissist entails

What is and is not feasible

How to establish limits

The Experience of Living with a Narcissist

A narcissist's primary concern is enhancing their sense of self-worth. It is possible to view narcissism as a self-esteem disease in which narcissists constantly struggle with feelings of relevance, importance, and status.

Although they could project confidence on the outside, they always question their deservingness. Their worth is behind the surface of assurance.

In essence, nothing and no one can ever be more significant than the enhancement and value of their sense of self. That covers everyone in a relationship they are engaged with.

When a narcissist experiences a decline in self-esteem, they are left with two choices:

They experience depression. They suffer from self-hatred, sadness, and everything, and everyone is surrounded by the aura that goes along with it.

They get haughty and start to claim they are unique, unbeatable, and flawless—all at the expense of you and others. They denigrate those around them to regain their sense of significance.

Naturally, they will select option number two, and as mentioned earlier, for them to feel important again, the person closest to them—that is, you—will most likely be discounted.

Narcissists are emotionally insensitive; they don't care when they harm you. They don't give a damn and most likely don't even notice how you respond to hurtful things said or done to you.

When you complain or say they have harmed you, they don't acknowledge it. They'll contest that your damaged feelings result from anything they've said or done. Most certainly, you are to blame. You might have heard the phrase "you're too sensitive" a lot, or they might accuse you of forcing you to say or behave a specific way.

This implies that the narcissist will continuously damage your feelings—whether by design or by mistake. You should be ready for this because it is a normal aspect of being in a relationship with a narcissist, and you won't be able to get away from their insensitivity or receive an apology.

Narcissists are unable to view themselves and other people realistically. According to Greenberg (2017), "whole object relations" refers to the capacity to recognize and accept a person's good and bad traits.

In early childhood, children learn to see the positive and negative aspects of people by seeing and imitating their parents. They also learn that their parents love and accept them despite their flaws.

This is attainable if an individual with NPD has the right psychotherapy and is motivated.

Individuals with non-whole object relations (NPD) who switch between two extreme perspectives of themselves and other people are either:

Exemplary, unique, unbeatable, and entitled (i.e., all-good), or

Garbage that is flawed, worthless, and defective (all bad)

The narcissist is incapable of viewing you as their partner in a steady and grounded way. Everyone has the opinion that they are either "special" or "worthless," and depending on how they are feeling at the time, they will switch between these two perspectives on themselves and other people (Greenberg, 2017).

This has nothing to do with you and isn't based on your actions.

The narcissist most likely saw you as flawless, unique, and perfect when your relationship was just getting started, the ideal of being all-good.

As the relationship progressed and they got to know you better, they noticed your flaws (which are universal) and how you weren't like their ideal partner. They would sometimes view you as very defective or completely awful.

There is only fleeting satisfaction; the narcissist's lack of "whole object relations" will eventually manifest itself. This will impact the relationship's happiness quotient and make whatever happiness you two may experience in the future brittle and fleeting.

Because narcissists are unable to maintain a positive, stable image of you, especially when they feel wounded, angry, dissatisfied, or disappointed by you, happiness is susceptible to being unexpectedly shaken (Greenberg, 2017).

They don't exhibit "object constancy," which essentially means that as soon as your narcissistic partner experiences something unpleasant, all that is positive vanishes, and any positive connection is severed.

Your positive past with them and all you've ever done for them is now completely erased and beyond their awareness. In your state of confusion, you wonder how this switch came about. Your partner may loathe you in a minute after you've experienced complete love, closeness, and happiness in the previous minute.

They don't have entire object relations, which is the cause of their complete about-face in terms of object constancy.

Recognize that people can only swing between loving and loathing you if they cannot view you, recognize your positive and negative qualities and behaviors, and accept you as an entire person.

These conflicting emotions depend on which of your traits or actions—the ones they like or dislike—are in evidence at the time.

This kind of changeover would occur, for instance, when you and your partner spend a lovely evening together without the children, who spend the evening with their grandparents. After preparing supper, you decide to watch a movie together. At home, it's a "date night."

It was a delicious dinner. The food was excellent, and you two had a great conversation about potential future travel destinations you both wanted to take the family.

After supper, you'd rather tidy the kitchen before seeing the movie, so you won't have to worry about it afterward. When you're done in the kitchen, tell your friend you'll be ready to watch the movie in a few minutes.

Unbeknownst to you, your narcissistic partner is starting to act inconsistently in their thoughts, believing that you are ruining their evening by cleaning the kitchen right before they are about to watch a movie. Your partner is irritated that they must wait for you instead of dropping everything and going out to see the movie.

Stepping outside, you settle into the couch, eager to start the movie and carry on with your partner on this romantic evening. By now, though, your partner is furious with you for being so thoughtless as to make them wait to see the film. They explain how your lack of consideration and rudeness gives them the impression that you don't love them or your time together.

It's unbelievable that this happens when you complete the simplest tasks, like tidying up the kitchen and cleaning up afterward. You find it unacceptable to be accused of being thoughtless and uncaring when, in reality, you have always supported your partner.

You are already aware of the prevalence of this kind of circumstance and how it has affected you if you are in a relationship with a narcissist. If you intend to date a narcissist, you should be aware of and ready for the kind of circumstance that was just explained. It is inevitable and inescapable because you are a different person than your mate.

This indicates that you are unique and possess a vastly distinct range of emotions and sensitivities. Innocent behavior that you observe could set off your narcissistic partner's insecurities. Everything that makes you feel happy and comfortable vanishes. Now that you've upset your narcissistic partner, they start to minimize you.

You're shocked by your narcissistic partner's abrupt 180-degree change in attitude and demeanor when they're busy venting their rage at you. Everything was OK a short while ago, but now there's a dispute where you must defend yourself against baseless and ludicrously unfair charges.

Chapter 2: Identifying Narcissistic Conduct

As was previously established, narcissism manifests itself in varying degrees. Thus, realizing this is the first step in identifying narcissistic behavior in yourself and others.

First, there is a degree of narcissism that is adaptive. Since this degree of narcissism is healthy, narcissistic personality disorder is not brought on by it. Being an adaptive narcissist makes you self-assured, self-confident, and inclined to self-care as part of your overall wellness regimen.

Maladaptive narcissism is another, and it manifests in many forms as well. Pathological levels of narcissism can negatively impact relationships, happiness, and overall well-being.

Essentially, the indications and manifestations of pathological narcissism will be the focus of our discussion.

It is important to note that the best method for identifying and diagnosing clinical narcissism is patient.

You should get a professional opinion as soon as possible if you observe the following traits or behaviors in yourself or someone you care about

#: You Adore Your Mirror A Little Too Much.

We discussed the story of Narcissus and how he could not look away from his reflection after getting a glimpse of it. He eventually withered away in front of a pool of water; some accounts claim he drowned. We noted how the story relates to NDP by pointing out that this is where the term "narcissism" first appeared in definition.

It may be considered narcissistic behavior if you find yourself fascinated by your reflection in the mirror and find yourself unable to go past one without pausing to acknowledge and appreciate your beauty.

It's important to note that there is nothing wrong with praising yourself or checking your appearance in front of the mirror. The type of self-enthrallment we are discussing here is the maladaptive kind that results in an obsession with your image. Obsessions of this nature give rise to unwholesome belief systems and self-images.

Magnificence

One of the main characteristics of pathological narcissism is grandiosity. It frequently comes across as having a conceited, unhealthy sense of self-importance that is unfounded. The kind in question is the unrealistic form of grandiosity that goes beyond a reasonable degree of confidence to the point of being conceited and conceited.

If you have a narcissistic personality, you'll think that you're unique and that no one else can compare to or surpass you. Additionally, you probably think that since you are "special," hanging out with people who are "below you" is beneath you. As a result of this notion, you will make a special effort to associate with people you consider to be your peers. These will typically be high-status individuals, objects, and locations.

You may also expect people to treat you a certain way if you have an exaggerated sense of grandeur and think you are the "best" or superior to everyone else. For example, you are likely to expect respect or admiration from others even if you have done nothing deserving. This need for approval will also probably lead you to exaggerate, if not outright lie, about your skills and accomplishments.

Furthermore, every interaction you have will probably revolve around how wonderful you are since you must ensure that others think highly of you. For example, when discussing work initiatives, you will emphasize how much you helped an endeavor succeed. You won't feel obliged to acknowledge other people's contributions. The main motivation behind this is to demonstrate your "amazingness" so that people—even your loved ones—will treat you like a celebrity and feel honored to have you in their lives.

#: Taking Responsibility Even When You Are at Fault

You can also utilize the trait of shifting blame to identify narcissistic behavior in yourself and others, even when you are the one at fault.

As was previously noted, narcissists get extremely defensive in the face of criticism since it goes against their false sense of self and "glorified" ego. They so tend to offend quickly, particularly in intimate relationships.

Above all, if you are a narcissist, you will assign blame or criticize the person expressing the viewpoint or criticism if it conflicts with your delusional self-image. For example, when your significant other confides in you about feeling abandoned, you are prone to assign blame, maybe by emphasizing the extent of your support.

Shifting the responsibility, even when you are at fault, makes it difficult to engage in self-criticism, which in turn makes engaging in self-growth difficult. Accepting responsibility is a problem when shifting blame.

Relationship problems arise in your personal and professional life when you cannot be accountable for your actions and behaviors. Being open to growth is essential for success in these areas of your life, and this can only occur when you are willing to take ownership of your actions and are self-critical.

People won't want to work with you or be in a committed relationship if you can't accept your flaws or limitations. Ignoring criticism from your loved ones will also make them feel ignored and unheard, which will strain your relationships even more.

#: There Are No Bounds to Your Obsession With Your Outer Image

A common trait of narcissistic people is a mad fixation with their image. It's not unreasonable to think that Narcissus's concern with his appearance would be unmatched if he had lived in the present era. In reality, he died gazing at a reflection of his face because he grew so fixated on his outward beauty that he was unable to stop staring at it.

Developing even a small level of self-awareness will show you that you spend a lot of money on self-grooming if you have a narcissistic personality. More than you can afford, at times. You spend this money to give the impression that you are from a higher social class. You will also observe that you your appearance.

According to a 2008 study by SimineVazire et al., identifying someone with narcissistic traits was not too difficult for an atypical observer. They disclosed that narcissistic individuals have particular tastes in jewelry, cosmetics, and attire. For instance, they probably prefer name-brand clothing and accessories.

The studies found that narcissistic guys are more likely to exhibit flamboyant dress sense in particular. Conversely, women are more likely to apply "loud" cosmetics and display excessive cleavage.

These results align with all that we have already covered regarding narcissistic conduct. Your wardrobe choices are likely to reflect your narcissistic tendencies, as you are obsessed with seeming 'high-status,' and you want people to notice and recognize you for who you are.

Section Three

Seeing Self-Centered Behaviour

Because narcissist is so attached to their absurd self-image, they will display traits that are exclusive to the disease. First, their body language will convey an air of superiority, arrogance, conceit, or snobbery. They will also act more important than they are, lie about things they have accomplished that they have not, and have an unbelievable overconfidence.

The Narcissist Owns All Rights To Bragging

They truly are tremendous braggarts. Their boasting can be subtly and deceptively done to avoid being exposed to exaggerations. They can excel at the "skill" of boasting. There will be a definite and persistent boasting. Even if they can demonstrate their accomplishments, they will always inflate the significance of their proof. Even if they do not know the issue, they will always act as an authority.

The Magical Mind of the Narcissist

The narcissist will occasionally exhibit what is known as magical thinking regarding how amazing they are, what they know, and what they are capable of. Sometimes, even in the face of overwhelming evidence to the contrary, they will even believe something to be true or accurate simply because they feel it is. When a narcissist sees that they clearly cannot "measure up" to someone else, they frequently become envious and try to minimize the other person by showing contempt and criticism.

The Arrogant Self-Hassler

The narcissist believes that they have the right to all they desire and that everything in life should proceed as they choose. They should receive the best care possible everywhere they go, and everyone should respect their desires, methods, and ways of thinking. In the narcissist's unique universe, they are always the special ones in the relationship, and if the noncomplier doesn't fit in, they will be labeled as difficult, stupid, and awkward.

The Deceitful Narcissist

Other people are frequently coerced into a submissive role by their employment, spouse, or children. Alternatively, the other person may occasionally just be too timid or fearful to question the narcissist's authority and will. Every time a narcissist enters a new relationship, they assume the other person is in a submissive role, even though this isn't the case. This makes it easy for the narcissist to take advantage of anyone unlucky enough to be in this situation.

Narcissists with Diverse Colours

These actions and viewpoints characterize the narcissist's mental state. There might be several levels of severity for the illness. Some narcissists wind up broken, alone, and unable to participate in society as a result of their extremely problematic social and familial interactions. Others may become extremely successful in business or at the pinnacle of their extremely demanding professions by mastering manipulation strategies and techniques to the point where they eventually gather an "entourage" of subordinates who attend to their every need, stroke their ego, swallow their pride, and typically take their very large paychecks to the bank. However, narcissists typically fall short in one area of life. Because they only love themselves, they cannot maintain partnerships in which love dictates behavior. They "forever gazing into the pool at their reflection" share a lifelong love affair.

Fundamental Ideas On Narcissism

Although narcissism is commonly perceived as self-centered, it is more nuanced than that. Both medical professionals and laypeople characterize narcissists as having an exaggerated sense of self. It's accurate. Narcissists have a very high opinion of themselves. The issue lies in that the self-being discussed here isn't fully formed.

A core self does not exist in narcissists.

The best illustrations of this mismatch are the mergers. They are forced to surround themselves with individuals they consider gifted, attractive, successful, and highly favorable characteristics. A narcissistic mother could take pride in her child's accomplishments. All the other wonderful things from the past will be forgotten once that gifted child stumbles and falls.

Conversely, those who are antisocial will simply distance themselves from the rest of society in order to avoid the disappointment of rejection or lack of admiration.

Narcissists' emotions fluctuate based on how you react to them.

When you first encounter a narcissist, you can't help but be impressed by his exuberance and seeming passion for life. Except for being antisocial, they are endearing and amiable. But once you've interacted with them a few times over time, you will begin to see some flaws.

If you disagree with everything the narcissist says, he will begin to display his true colors. At best, he will begin to pout, and at worst, he will become verbally aggressive.

Narcissus can produce other narcissists.

Additionally, narcissistic parenting can produce narcissism. Some parents are so focused on themselves that their kids must resort to self-preservation techniques. These kids could develop wildly imaginative backstories due to their defense mechanisms. They, in other words, turn into narcissists.

The same conclusion may also be reached by narcissistic parents who adore their kids because they believe they are too special to bear children. The kids will accept their parents' extravagant justifications since they are overindulged and spoiled.

But pay attention to how the term "can" is used. It's also possible that a narcissistic parent's child can overcome this mistreatment and come out bruised but not broken.

All people were narcissists at first.

A real human must first love himself enough to give it a shot. The impulses of survival are selfish. A newborn is indifferent to the emotions of others. It cannot still reflect and think. But it already understands that it needs warm, cozy clothing, food, water, and shelter to survive. Fortunately, a baby's parents or other guardians will comfort him or her when she cries.

A certain amount of narcissism is necessary for a child's growth in order to help him recognize his value. But narcissists can never fully get rid of their infantile state. They have not grown to truly empathize with others; instead, they still follow their survival instincts.

But narcissists are not born; they are made.

The good news is that no one has the personality disorder from birth, even though everyone requires a certain amount of narcissism. What makes a narcissist who they are is a result of their experiences in life. The fact that some of them are abuse survivors is regrettable. It's also possible that they are unintentionally imparting these traits to their kids.

Certain narcissistic subtypes cause more harm to other people.

Not every narcissist is the same. Some narcissists are seen as dangerous. Malignant narcissism is more than just a case of arrogance or pride. It continues to wreak havoc on other people's lives, becoming so nasty and hateful that there are instances when running is the only option.

www.ingramcontent.com/pod-product-compliance
Lightning Source LLC
Chambersburg PA
CBHW052152110526
44591CB00012B/1958